PETER LAFFERTY is a former secondary school science teacher. Since 1985 he has been a full-time author of science and technology books for children and family audiences, and has written over 50 books. He has edited and contributed to many scientific encyclopedias and dictionaries.

BETTY ROOT was the Director of the Reading and Language Information Centre at the University of Reading in England for over twenty years. She has worked on numerous children's books, both fiction and non-fiction.

SHIRLEY WILLIS was born in Glasgow, Scotland. She has worked as an illustrator, designer and editor, mainly on books for children.

BOOK EDITOR: KAREN BARKER
TECHNICAL CONSULTANT: PETER LAFFERTY
LANGUAGE CONSULTANT: BETTY ROOT

AN SBC BOOK, CONCEIVED, EDITED AND DESIGNED BY THE SALARIYA BOOK COMPANY, 25, MARLBOROUGH PLACE, BRIGHTON, EAST SUSSEX BN1 1UB, UNITED KINGDOM.
© THE SALARIYA BOOK COMPANY LTD MCMXCVIII

PUBLISHED IN 1999 IN THE UNITED STATES BY FRANKLIN WATTS
AN IMPRINT OF SCHOLASTIC INC.
557 BROADWAY, NEW YORK, NY 10012
PUBLISHED SIMULTANEOUSLY IN CANADA.

ISBN 978 0 531 11831 3 (LIB. BDG.)
ISBN 978 0 531 15981 1 (PBK.)

VISIT FRANKLIN WATTS ON THE INTERNET AT: HTTP://PUBLISHING.GROLIER.COM

Library of Congress Cataloging-in-Publication Data
Willis, Shirley.
    Tell me why planes have wings / Shirley Willis.
    p.   cm. – (Whiz kids) Includes index.
    Summary: Text and simple illustrations provide explanations of the principles of flight.
    ISBN 0 531 11831 2
    1. Aerodynamics – Juvenile literature. 2. Flight – Juvenile literature. 3. Airplanes – Juvenile literature.
    [1. Aerodynamics. 2. Flight. 3. Airplanes.]
    I. Title II. Series: Whiz kids (Series)
TL547.W644 1999   629.132'3 – dc21
                        98-33580 CIP AC

GROLIER PUBLISHING

PRINTED IN SHANGHAI, CHINA.
REPRINTED IN 2012.
16 17 18 19 20 R 12

WHIZ KIDS

CONTENTS

Wherever you see this sign, ask an adult to help you.

WHIZ KIDS
TELL ME WHY PLANES HAVE WINGS

SHIRLEY WILLIS

W
FRANKLIN WATTS

A Division of Grolier Publishing
NEW YORK • LONDON • HONG KONG • SYDNEY
DANBURY, CONNECTICUT

FLYING LOOKS EASY!

CAN I FLY?

You cannot fly
because the
force of gravity
pulls you toward
the ground. ?

6

In order to fly,
the force of gravity
has to be overcome.

Birds, bats, and insects can fly because they can overcome gravity.

BUZZ
BUZZ

7

GRAVITY KEEPS YOUR FEET ON THE GROUND!

WHAT IS GRAVITY?

The force of gravity keeps you on the ground.
Without gravity you would float.

8

When something falls — like this apple — it is being pulled down by gravity.

BOING!

You cannot see gravity, but it pulls everything toward the center of Earth.

9

How Do Birds Fly?

Birds can fly because they can overcome gravity.

A bird's bones are hollow,
so its body is not very heavy.
By flapping its wings,
a bird lifts itself
off the ground
and starts to fly.

A bird's body is built for flying.
It has strong muscles to flap its wings and lightweight feathers to protect it from the cold.

11

CAN YOU STOP GRAVITY?

READY, GET SET, GO!

You cannot stop gravity, but air can slow down its effect.

A PAPER RACE

Take two sheets of paper. Crumple one sheet into a ball. Now drop them both together from the same height.

The paper ball falls faster because it is smaller. The sheet traps more air underneath it. This slows it down as it falls.

12

How To Make A Parachute

You will need:

A plastic bag
Scissors
A ruler
4 pieces of string
(each 1 foot long)
Adhesive tape
Plasticine

1. With help from an adult, cut a 1-foot square from a plastic bag.

2. Tape a piece of string to each corner, as shown.

3. Knot the loose ends together and press into a blob of plasticine.

When an object falls, air acts like a brake to slow it down.

This is called drag.

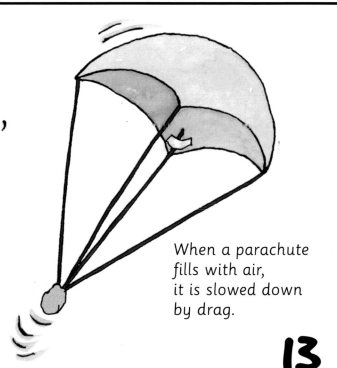

When a parachute fills with air, it is slowed down by drag.

13

WHAT IS AIR?

Air is a mixture of invisible gases, and it is all around us.

When air moves from one place to another, it is called wind.

Wind is moving air.

Warm air rises and cold air sinks. As warm air rises, cold air rushes into the empty space below. This is wind.

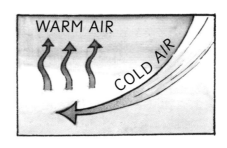

You cannot see wind
but you can feel it
blowing against you.
On a windy day
you can see it
blowing trees, flags,
and clothes drying
on a clothesline.

15

DO PLANES FLOAT IN THE AIR?

A glider is a plane without an engine.

YOU CAN SEE GLIDERS, BUT YOU CAN'T HEAR THEM.

Gliders float on rising currents of warm air called thermals.

A glider pilot must follow warm-air thermals to stay in the air.

DOES WARM AIR REALLY RISE?

You will need:
A sheet of stiff paper
Scissors
A pencil
Yarn
Felt-tip pens

1. Draw a spiral on the paper.
   Now color it in to
   look like a snake.
2. With help from an adult,
   cut around the spiral.
3. Now thread the yarn
   through the snake's head.
   Knot it underneath.

Now hang your "snake"
above a radiator and watch
it spin. Rising warm air is
making it turn.

17

Do You Need Wings To Fly?

Planes, birds, bats, and insects all need wings to fly.
But you can fly without wings in a hot-air balloon.

Bubbles rise because they are full of warm air. As the air inside begins to cool, the bubbles start to fall.

18

Hot air rises
because it is
lighter than
cold air.
A hot-air balloon
will float upward
if the air inside it
is heated.

19

WHY DO PLANES HAVE WINGS?

A plane needs wings to fly.

When a plane speeds along a runway, air rushes past. As the air rushes over and under the wings, the plane rises off the ground.

The upward force is called lift.

20

A plane's wings are flat underneath and curved on top.
This shape is called an airfoil.
This special shape lifts the wings and pulls the plane upward.

WE NEED AIRFOIL-SHAPED ARMS!

HOW DO PLANES STAY UP?

IT'S TIME FOR LIFTOFF!

The lift of a plane's wings pulls it up into the sky and keeps it there.

WHOOSH!

Engines propel a plane forward at great speed. This is called thrust. If a plane stopped moving forward, it would quickly drop from the sky.

HOW TO MAKE A PAPER PLANE

1. Fold a sheet of paper in half.

2. Now fold two corners toward the center as shown.

3. Fold toward the center again.

4. Now fold in half and fold the wings back.

5. It's time for takeoff!

23

How Do Planes Go So Fast?

A plane needs an engine to go fast.

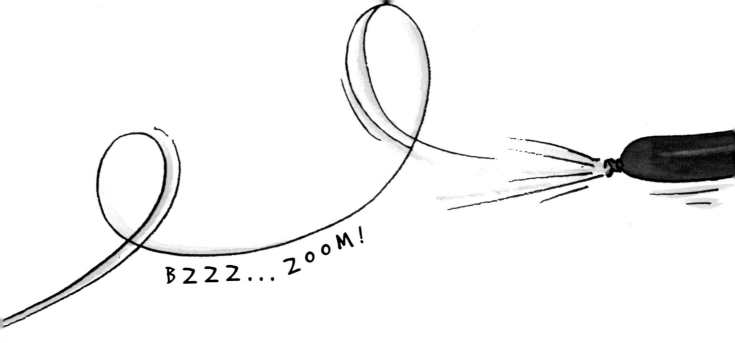

BZZZ...ZOOM!

A JET-PROPELLED BALLOON

Blow up a balloon and let it go.
A jet of air shoots out and
propels the balloon
through the air.

Jet engines make planes go very fast.
A blast of gases rushes from the back
of a jet engine and thrusts the plane
forward at great speed.

HOW DO YOU STEER A PLANE?

A pilot turns a plane by tilting its rudder left or right. The pilot raises or lowers special flaps on the wings and tailplanes to go up or down.

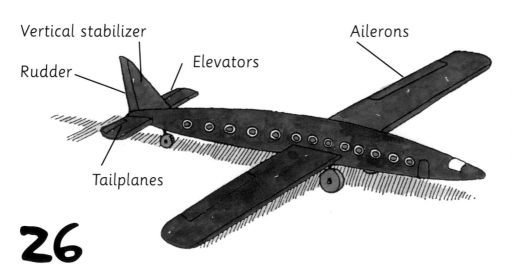

Vertical stabilizer

Rudder

Elevators

Ailerons

Tailplanes

The wing flaps are called ailerons. The flaps on the tailplanes are called elevators.

27

CAN PLANES FLY BACKWARD?

A helicopter can fly backward or forward. It can also fly up, down, or sideways.

Spin the stick quickly between your hands and throw it into the air. Watch the whirligig fly.

HOW TO MAKE A WHIRLIGIG

You will need:

A plastic bottle
A thin stick
Scissors
A felt-tip pen
A ruler

1. Measure out a rectangle (8in x 2in) on a plastic bottle. Now cut it out.
2. Mark the middle of the rectangle. Cut a slit on either side, as shown.
3. Make a hole in the middle just big enough to push the stick through.
4. Press the blades down slightly, as shown.

Helicopters have spinning rotor blades instead of wings. The spinning blades lift the helicopter straight up into the air.

GLOSSARY

ailerons   Movable flaps on a plane's wings that help it move up or down.

airfoil   A special shape that creates an upward force called lift. Helicopter blades and airplane wings are airfoil-shaped.

elevators   Movable flaps on the tailplanes that help a plane move up or down.

gravity   The force that pulls objects toward the center of Earth.

helicopter   An aircraft that has spinning blades instead of wings.

hot-air balloon   A huge balloon that is filled with hot air to make it rise.

jet engine   An aircraft engine that thrusts hot gases backward.

lift   An upward force that overcomes the pull of gravity.

parachute   A device that balloons out like an umbrella as it falls through the air. It helps people land safely on the ground.

plane   An airplane; a flying machine with wings.

propel   To make something move forward.

rudder   A movable flap on a plane's vertical stabilizer to make it turn.

tailplanes   The small back wings of a plane.

thermals   Currents of rising warm air used by gliders to fly.

thrust   The force from the engines that propels a plane through the air.

vertical stabilizer   The upright fin at the back of the plane.

INDEX